Favorite
CLASSICAL
Melodies

TRUMPET

Arranged and Recorded by David Pearl
("Brandenburg Concerto No. 5, First Movement" arranged and recorded by Donald Sosin)

Cherry Lane Music Company
Director of Publications/Project Supervisor: Mark Phillips

ISBN: 978-1-60378-415-3

Visit our website at www.cherrylaneprint.com

CONTENTS

AVE MARIA

By Charles Gounod and Johann Sebastian Bach

TRUMPET

Moderately slow

BRANDENBURG CONCERTO NO. 5, FIRST MOVEMENT

By Johann Sebastian Bach

TRUMPET

CARO MIO BEN

TRUMPET

By Giuseppe Giordani

CLAIR DE LUNE

TRUMPET

By Claude Debussy

FUNERAL MARCH OF A MARIONETTE

TRUMPET

by Charles Gounod

Moderately fast, in 2

9

GYMNOPÉDIE NO. 1

TRUMPET

By Erik Satie

HALLELUJAH CHORUS

from *Messiah*

By George Frideric Handel

TRUMPET

HUNGARIAN DANCE NO. 5

TRUMPET

By Johannes Brahms

Moderately

Slower

Tempo I

MINUET
(from String Quintet in E Major)

By Luigi Boccherini

TRUMPET

Moderately

PIANO SONATA NO. 14 "MOONLIGHT"

First Movement

TRACK 10

TRUMPET

By Ludwig van Beethoven

Slowly

Piano

Play

poco rit.   a tempo

SYMPHONY NO. 5

First Movement

TRUMPET

By Ludwig van Beethoven

Moderately fast

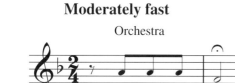

WILLIAM TELL OVERTURE

TRUMPET

By Gioacchino Rossini

Moderately fast

POMP AND CIRCUMSTANCE

TRUMPET

By Edward Elgar

Moderately

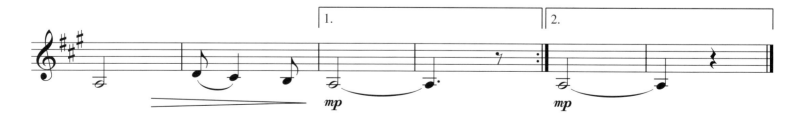